collective

Contemporary Styles Series

CD INCLUDED

Fusion: A Study in Conte...
Music for the Bass

by Leo Traversa

thecollective is a world-class learning center for drumset players, percussionists, bassists, keyboardists and guitarists of all levels. We offer plans of study ranging from individual lessons and clinics to full-time programs of ten weeks to two years in length. If you're serious about becoming the best musician you can be, we're serious about helping you accomplish that goal.

**541 Avenue of the Americas,
New York, NY 10011
T: 212-741-0091**

www.thecoll.com

Executive Producer – *Lauren Keiser*
Executive Co-producer – *John Costellano*
Author Liason – *Tony Maggiolino*
Creative Director – *Alex Teploff*
Managing Editor – *Nicholas Hopkins*
Production Editor – *Seth Goldberg*
Cover Design – *Andrew J. Dowty*
Book Design – *Andrew J. Dowty*
Production Designer – *Andy Ray Wong*
Photo of New York City – *Maureen Plainfield*
Other Photography – *Andy Dowty and Kyung Chul-Choi*
Production Coordinator and Audio Engineer – *Tony Conniff*

CARL FISCHER®

65 Bleecker Street, New York, NY 10012

ISBN 0-8258-6266-3

TABLE OF CONTENTS

Performers on the CD:

Ol' Factory
Drums: Kim Plainfield
Guitar: Burr Johnson
Bass: Al Payson

Q and *I Was Walkin'*
Drums: Kim Plainfield
Piano: Bob Quaranta
Bass: Leo Traversa

Monte Cristo
Drums: Kim Plainfield
Piano: Bob Quaranta
Bass: Lincoln Goines

FOREWORD

The Collective was established in 1977 by a small group of professional New York musicians, who wanted to pool their energies and create a place where young drummers, and later bass, guitar, and keyboard students, could study and prepare themselves for a career in music. Since opening its doors, The Collective has graduated thousands of students, who have gone on to establish themselves in the world of professional music. I don't think that it is immodest to say that our alumni are helping to shape the direction that popular music is taking around the world.

Over the years the curriculum at The Collective has evolved to include a wide range of courses focusing on everything from technique and reading, to the study of all the important contemporary and ethnic styles. This book, along with our other Rhythm Section based books, covers the material offered in the Collective's Certificate Program.

The styles offered here represent the key styles in the contemporary idiom. Since all styles have tended to grow out of each other, and mutually influence each other, the student will find common threads that link them all together and make it easier to absorb and make them part of a young musician's personal style signature.

Each book contains a brief biography of the author, who is the faculty member who teaches this style at The Collective. You will also find a brief introduction to the general style and examples of the various substyles to be studied. Woven throughout the material are performance tips that come out of the teacher's years of experience. The most important element, however, are the pre-recorded rhythm-section CDs, on which our teachers perform with other musicians who also specialize in playing the style. Listening to and practicing with these CDs are the most important things for you to do to develop skills playing in the style. Music notation and the written word can, at best, only help you derive an intellectual understanding of the music. It is in listening to the actual music that you will come to understand it. In this regard, we strongly encourage you to make an effort to listen to the music listed in the recommended discography at the end of each section. The blank staves are meant for you to notate your own personal variations for each style. First, you must learn the pure style; then, you can adapt it to your own musical needs.

I would like to express my appreciation to all the teachers who have, over the years, contributed to the growth of the Collective and to this program in particular. I would also like to thank the hard working and talented folks at Carl Fischer for supporting our effort to get it right, and doing such a fine job with this book. Finally, I would like to thank Tony Maggiolino of our staff for all his hard work in coordinating all the material, and struggling to meet ever looming deadlines.

—John Castellano.
Director, The Collective

Author's Introduction

This book was conceived at The Collective in New York City by a longtime friend and colleague of mine, Kim Plainfield. Kim and I have shared the stage with Tania Maria, Jon Lucien, Dave Kikoski and many others and have also performed together at The Collective in classes, faculty concerts and on the twenty-fifth anniversary DVD. Our collaborations have many times, been in the genres of Fusion music, especially the fusion of Afro-Cuban, and Brazilian styles with jazz, rock and funk. Here we give you four examples of those styles, true hybrid grooves that bridge musical genres and cultures to give you a new sound and rhythm to experiment with.

The concept of the book was not only to teach different styles through compositions, but to give players the tools, through exercises and examples that you will need to become proficient in the various genres necessary to play fusion music. Each style of music is like a language with its own alphabet and its own vocabulary that you must learn before you can communicate comfortably. The exercises are designed to make it easier for you to execute the bass parts in the original compositions included in the book, as played by myself and two other well-known and respected New York bassists, Lincoln Goines and Al Payson. As you learn the music, we encourage you to be creative and elaborate on the parts already given or create your own parts. As you play along with the CD, you'll be accompanied by Kim and Bob Quaranta, who is incomparable and invaluable for his work at The Collective, as well as Burr Johnson on guitar in the last piece. Bob and Burr also composed two of the compositions we used here. In some ways, it is almost like being in a rhythm section class at The Collective, where you would indeed have opportunities to play with some of the top New York City professionals from the faculty and outside of the school as well, in different settings playing different styles.

I hope you will enjoy the music and be inspired to explore these styles even more. Good luck!

—Leo Traversa

About Leo Traversa

Bassist Leo Traversa is a founding and current faculty member of the Collective in New York City, and has taught at the Collective since 1987. His extensive knowledge of a variety of musical genres and cultures as well as his mastery of their playing techniques makes him one of the most versatile and proficient bassists on the scene today. In addition to his experience in the field of music education, he has performed, toured and recorded with a wide range of internationally known artists. These include Tania Maria, Ben E. King, Astrud Gilberto, Michael Brecker, Don Byron, Cesar Camargo Mariano, Dave Valentin, Toninho Horta, Gerry Mulligan, The New York Voices, Oscar Castro Nieves, Eliane Elias, Oscar Hernandez, Phil Woods, Eileen Ivers, The Caribbean Jazz Project, Steve Kimock, Gato Barbieri, Ivan Lins, Chris Wasburn's "Syotos" band, Aster Aweke, Dorothy Masuku and many others. He has led his own group of European musicians on several international tours and has also garnered many television, film, and Broadway credits during the span of his remarkable career.

CHAPTER 1:
[I Was Walkin']

This song is in $\frac{3}{4}$ and for lack of any specific style label, I would call it a Afro/world/fusion beat in $\frac{3}{4}$. Because of a great interest I have in African music, my first instinct in the introduction and the A-sections took me towards the African side of the groove, specifically South African. Instead of choosing to articulate each note, I slide between the notes using octaves. This is something I learned while listening to African music. Every musician brings his or her lifetime experiences and influences to the table whenever we perform with others or are asked to interpret an original composition. As bassists, often, we are asked to create our own parts given a lead sheet and melody, or maybe just a page with the chords on it. So, what we should do next is to take a listen to the drummer, see how he is interpreting the song then listen to the overall song, in this case just a piano playing the melody and chords. Although the drums heavily influence your part (or you influence the drum part), you can extrapolate your parts from anywhere else in the music. A vocal or horn melody, rhythm part or accent can give you ideas. When getting ideas from the drums, it could be the bass drum/snare pattern or maybe just the hi-hat. If I feel that following the bass-drum part may be too busy or too syncopated and will be too busy, I may check out the hi-hat part and get an idea from that.

Here is the basic pattern (played on hi-hat, tom-toms, snare drum and bass drum) that is being played in the opening section:

Example 1. Drum Groove

From that, the basic foundation is this:

Example 2. Groove Basics

Here is the bass part extrapolated from the drums:

Example 3. Bass Part

The choice to use slides felt natural to fatten up the part and give it some flavor or spice. I considered a more sixteenth-note approach but felt it would take away from the African influence that I was feeling at the time. Playing bass parts using octaves is fairly common in many styles, and it's important to be comfortable in your left hand moving around the neck and shifting positions. This exercise is a study in octaves. Keep your left hand-position constant playing the lower octave with your first finger and the upper with your fourth. With your left hand constant, shift your hand position around the neck. If your fingering is good, you should be able to hit your targets with your first finger as your fourth follows naturally.

Example 4. Octave Exercise

Playing in this $\frac{3}{4}$ meter is interesting and fun, because it's not as common as other $\frac{3}{4}$ or $\frac{6}{8}$ rhythms we play more often. It has a straight eighth-note feel, as opposed to the $\frac{3}{4}$ swing feel we are probably more used to and is a little more wide open a groove than an Afro-Cuban $\frac{6}{8}$. Playing in $\frac{3}{4}$ or $\frac{6}{8}$ meter is very common in parts of the world like South America, Africa and parts of the Caribbean, but Americans and Westerners in general are not quite as used to it, except for waltzes and some Gospel music. It is important to feel other rhythms and get comfortable with them to expand your rhythmic vocabulary. Later on in the book, we'll cover the relationships between playing in 3 and 4.

The B-section of the song features dotted half notes playing the roots of the chords for five bars with accents in bars 6 and 7 and a unison figure in bar 8. Here, it's important to keep your place, counting if necessary, when you play the accents and the figure. Being in $\frac{3}{4}$ instead of $\frac{4}{4}$, you may not be able to get by feeling the beat like we can sometimes do in $\frac{4}{4}$. A common rehearsal tool is to "loop" the bars that may be difficult and repeat them over and over until mastered. Here is the loop of the last four bars of the B-section.

Example 5. Last Four Bars of the B-Section

The C-section is a sixteenth-note funk pattern. Here, I did use some sixteenth-note articulation. Here is the bass part.

Example 6. Bass Part at C

Sixteenth-note articulation has become a part of the language of Fusion music as well as Funk/Jazz and Latin styles since the days of Jaco Pastorius, Alfonso Johnson, Percy Jones and Francis Rocco Prestia, among others. Notice how the left and right hands work together to create the proper articulation or feel. Here is the part with the articulations, or in other words, slides and hammers notated.

Example 7. Bass Part with Articulations

It's important to mention some of the points about recording music in this setting; that is, a situation that calls for reading, knowledge of different styles, creativity and improvisational skills. First, have a basic game plan that you know will work. Establish a working groove concept that you feel comfortable with. Maybe later, you and the drummer or leader will elaborate on it or even change it but go in with a working plan to get the music started. If you are in a touring band, you may record something one way and then, after months of playing it live on the road, have a completely different approach. That's fairly common. Music is a constantly evolving entity. That's one of the things that is so great about it.

Now that I've mentioned it, let me give you an example from this song. In the piano solo at letter **E** there is a chord change per bar, and the harmony consists of fairly complex upper structure chords. Not wanting to get in the way, I chose to play long and low roots to establish the harmony and allow the pianist room to play his solo. However, in retrospect, a more sixteenth-note approach would have also worked, to build up to the straight sixteenth notes at the end of the solo. Recording Jazz usually has its moments like that, where you have many options and aren't quite sure witch is the best, even after you've recorded. So, to make amends and for my own personal satisfaction, here is a sixteenth-note part based on the piano-solo section.

Example 8. Alternate Solo Part

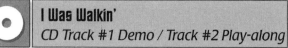
I Was Walkin'
CD Track #1 Demo / Track #2 Play-along

I Was Walkin'

KIM PLAINFIELD and
LINCOLN GOINES

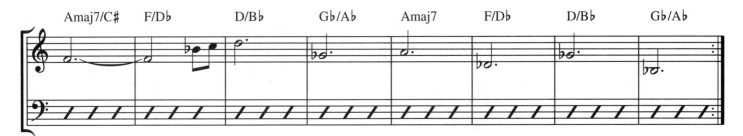

Chart Roadmap

Intro (4x), A (7x), A, B, C, Intro, A (7x), A, B, C, D E, F, G(3x), H

CHAPTER 2:
[Q]

Q is a very interesting composition by Bob Quaranta. This song is a wonderful example of the influence of African rhythms and how they can be blended with Jazz harmony quite successfully. It's also a lesson on how to interpret Afro-Cuban $\frac{6}{8}$ rhythms. One of the points that I continually stress in class is becoming comfortable with $\frac{6}{8}$ or $\frac{12}{8}$ rhythms as they relate to $\frac{4}{4}$. To play many West African, South American, Caribbean and Fusion styles, it's crucial to have an understanding of the different undercurrents of time that are taking place. $\frac{12}{8}$, $\frac{6}{8}$, $\frac{6}{4}$, $\frac{3}{4}$ and $\frac{3}{2}$ are all present within the $\frac{4}{4}$ foundation. One exercise that's helpful in establishing this concept is to play the different meters while tapping your foot or setting your metronome in $\frac{4}{4}$ time. Continue each one until you feel comfortable, then try to alternate between the different exercises until you're comfortable with that.

Here are some examples of what we're discussing. I'll try to show how the different meters line up with the $\frac{4}{4}$ base.

Example 13. $\frac{3}{2}$ over $\frac{4}{4}$

Think $\frac{12}{8}$ in three groups of four eighth notes.

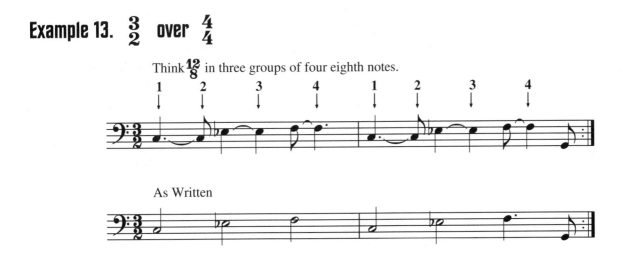

As Written

Q is written in $\frac{6}{8}$, but when I played it, I felt it in four and tapped my foot in four to make the opening accents strong and accurate. More specifically, every two of my quarter notes equaled one bar of $\frac{6}{8}$. However, the drummer was playing a more $\frac{6}{4}$ oriented feel on drums. Here's the drum part played on hi-hat, snare drum and bass drum:

Example 14. Drum Part

It is important to understand that in some situations, all these rhythms are happening at the same time. In West African styles, especially from Cameroon, Mali and Senegal, there are three to four meters happening simultaneously. In music from Columbia and Venezuela as well as the Netherlands Antilles, there is a mixture of meters within the $\frac{3}{4}$ meter. It's very interesting music and after practice, you'll acquire greater ease in feeling the time naturally.

The opening bars of *Q* are syncopated accents in $\frac{6}{8}$. They are on the tricky side of things, so accuracy and attack are very important in the proper execution. For myself, to make that happen, I felt more comfortable thinking in 4s; that is, feeling a $\frac{4}{4}$ pulse with triplets. When performing or recording, it's always best to do what's right for you to perform your best. It may not be what's best for someone else, but making the music the best it can be is the most important thing. Therefore, I'm all for doing whatever it takes to make that happen. This would be a good section to loop when rehearsing, so using your metronome, see if you can play the figure accurately several times. Then try it with the rest of the band.

Example 15. Intro Figure in $\frac{6}{8}$

After the intro figure, there is a break for the melody pickup at letter A, followed by dotted quarter notes and then the second part of the intro figure. This part was written in $\frac{6}{8}$, and concentration is paramount, because the bars in $\frac{6}{8}$ go by very quickly at this tempo. Letter **A** is repeated, which brings us to letter **B**. This is a kind of release where the tension and syncopation of letter A smooth out and the song opens up a bit. This is reflected in the more open bass part that supports the melody.

On to letter **C**, where the solos begin on a different form, starting with piano. But before we go on, let's explore the reality of a typical bass player's world.

As a faculty member at the Bass Collective, one of the things that I have always stressed to students in my classes and lessons was the ability to create your own bass part from a rhythm and some chords. So often, in live performance situations and even recording situations, we are given a lead sheet and asked, using our knowledge of different rhythms and our knowledge of harmony and bass patterns, to create a bass part that suits and complements the song. (A lead sheet is a chart that has the melody written out with chord symbols above, like you would find in any common fake book.) Knowing that, you can see that the more you know about different styles and harmony, and the more vocabulary you have to draw from when asked to create a part, the easier it will be for you to do. Sometimes, your ideas may change the way even the composer thinks about the song. Music is the ultimate collaboration, and a good band leader or composer will take advantage of his or her musicians' knowledge to make the music as good as it can be.

In the solo section at letter **C**, the Afro-Cuban side of the $\frac{6}{8}$ is more apparent, and the bass part changes accordingly. Drawing on a typical Bembe kind of $\frac{6}{8}$, the bass is playing a part derived from the $\frac{6}{8}$ clave pattern. Having played and recorded with many Latin and Latin Jazz artists, this was natural to me, but it is also something important that all instrumentalists should become comfortable with.

Here is the basic rhythm for this kind of part in $\frac{6}{8}$. I've looped the first eight bars of letter **C** so you can repeat the feel for a while. If you have a drum machine, program a $\frac{6}{8}$ clave pattern and play this along to that.

Example 16. $\frac{6}{8}$ Clave

Example 17. Loops of the First 8 Bars of the Solo Section

Here is a more basic and typical $\frac{6}{8}$ part that you hear in many Afro Cuban $\frac{6}{8}$ situations and Latin Jazz songs like Afro Blue. Again, play this with the drum machine playing clave; even better, try to tap your foot in $\frac{4}{4}$ while playing it.

Example 18. Typical Afro-Cuban $\frac{6}{8}$ Bass Part

Here's a variation, with a little more clave in it.

Example 19. Afro-Cuban Bass Part with an Upbeat in the Second Bar

When playing in $\frac{3}{4}$, $\frac{6}{8}$ or $\frac{12}{8}$, it's very important to be able to relate it to $\frac{4}{4}$ and play it while feeling the 4, and even tapping your foot in 4. If you see dancers in Africa or Cuba dancing to $\frac{6}{8}$ rhythms, that is the pulse that they dance to. When playing some of the more complex African and South American rhythms, it will be a great help to relate to them in $\frac{4}{4}$. In some of my early experiences playing African music with Martino Atangana, a great guitarist from Cameroon, I would notice that although I was feeling the music in 3, his foot would always be going in 4. Later on, it really helped me because—and you may find out—that many musicians, especially in the world music genres, don't always count off a song. They just start playing and expect you to enter in the right place, so you will be much better off knowing where the various rhythms lies in relationship to $\frac{4}{4}$.

On this recording, a bass solo was requested, a nice but unexpected surprise. I tried to approach it with an African slant, playing some pentatonic riffs that also sound a bit bluesy. It's important, I feel, to have the vocabulary of the music you're playing at your disposal. What I mean is, instead of taking a purely jazz kind of approach to Latin Jazz or African-oriented music, try to include some elements of the native style, rhythmically and harmonically. It can help bridge the styles and make a more complete statement.

After the bass solo comes the drum solo, where bass and piano continue a figure to accompany the drum solo. I've been in many situations with Jazz groups and Latin groups as well as the great Brazilian artist Tania Maria where the rhythm section plays during the drum solo. This can get troublesome if you don't count, pay attention and trust your sense of time. If the drum or percussion soloist plays something that throws you off or if they stumble on a figure their trying out, you must stay solid. Otherwise, chaos will surely ensue.

Here we took the intro figure and put some space in it. Before you try to play along with the drum solo, try this (you will need a metronome or drum machine with a foot switch or another person with you). Set up a beat or just a pulse and play along to it, then turn off the metronome or drum machine and continue to play. While still playing, put the metronome or drum machine back on. See if you're still in the pocket. If you have someone else there, they can turn the volume down and up again for you to see if you can maintain good tempo.

Here's the figure for the drum solo.

Example 20. Drum Solo Figure

Here is the lead sheet that was used at the recording session. Make sure your bass part supports the melody both harmonically and rhythmically.

CD Track #3 Demo / Track #4 Play-along

ROBERT QUARANTA

Intro

Play 4 times

A

B 𝄋

Fine

To Solo (first time through form)
D.C. (second time through form)

Chart Roadmap
Intro, A, B, C(4x),D, B, Intro, A, B

CHAPTER 3:
(Monte Cristo)

Monte Cristo is a powerful composition by Lincoln Goines and Bill O'Connell. It is a solid example of the relationship between $\frac{6}{8}$ and $\frac{4}{4}$ starting out with an Afro-Cuban/Rock style $\frac{6}{8}$ followed by a $\frac{4}{4}$ Rock beat in E minor, followed by a contemporary Brazilian Baião variation and a contemporary Latin/Fusion groove. It may sound like a lot, but it all makes sense and flows together because all the rhythms used are related in time (pulse) and gradually get more syncopated as the song progresses. The opening $\frac{6}{8}$ section is based on the eighth-note triplet. The fourth time around the figure in bar 16, the figure slides smoothly into the second section in four, which is a basic Rock beat with little syncopation. All this is the introduction, until we arrive at letter **A**, still in the $\frac{4}{4}$ rock feel in E minor. The next section is a Baião variation witch gets more syncopated (Baião is a Brazilian rhythm originating in the north of Brazil.) Here, the bass is really interesting, adding a nice twist to the basic Baião pattern. Finally we arrive at the Latin section which is again more syncopated, enhanced even more by Lincoln's support of the piano part and later, some eighth-note variations.

As you can see, a thorough knowledge of different world styles as well as western styles is a must if you ever wish to play Jazz or Jazz-fusion styles. Many of these rhythms are also incorporated in today's pop and dance music as well. You can hear clave rhythms in all kinds of popular music from Techno House grooves to New Orleans styles. The universal African roots of our popular music are never too far away.

In the opening section, or introduction, there are triplets being played. Playing in groups of three and six brings up some interesting issues for the right hand. You must be more conscious of your right-hand fingering and articulate the groupings of three. One exercise I used to do to practice triplets was to play a chromatic scale but accent the first note of each triplet. Since the harmonic rhythm is strange, it forces you to really concentrate on the triplet.

Here it is. We'll start on G in third position. This can also be a good exercise to stretch your left hand when you do it down in the lower positions. The slower you play, the better the left-hand stretch.

Example 21. Chromatic Scale Starting on G in Triplets

Here's another exercise in triplet articulation.

Example 22.

You can alter any of your scale exercises to articulate triplets, for example, playing your scales three notes at a time.

Example 23. C-Major Scale in Triplets

Or your arpeggios in groups of three. This is a little trickier.

Example 24. C-Major Arpeggios in Triplets

To execute the beginning and end of *Monte Cristo,* you must have the ability to go between $\frac{6}{8}$ and $\frac{4}{4}$ comfortably and smoothly. To practice that, let's again use a loop. Here we've changed the pattern a little to create two 8-bar sections, one in $\frac{6}{8}$ and the other in 4 with the seventh bar of each section being the transition bar for the new time signature. As we've done before, let's keep our pulse in $\frac{4}{4}$, even when we're in $\frac{6}{8}$. This will help the transitions.

Example 25. Intro to Monte Cristo Loop

This transition is very common in Jazz, with some songs going from a jazz waltz $\frac{3}{4}$ to a $\frac{4}{4}$ swing, or a $\frac{6}{8}$ groove into $\frac{4}{4}$ swing. Some songs that can go between 6 and 4 or 4 and 3 are *Invitation, Waltz for Debbie, Milestones, A Night in Tunisia* and *Footprints.*

After the 16-bar E minor transition section, we arrive at letter **B**. The rhythm that the drums play here is called "Baião" from Brazil. Here is the basic pattern for a Baião for the bass.

Example 26. Basic Baião Pattern

Here is Lincoln's variation on it. The notes on the "and" of four and the "and" of one give it a unique feel. This is a great example of being creative and using your ideas while still supporting the band and laying down the groove.

Example 27. Lincoln's Variation

Letter **C** sets up a "songo." Songo is a pattern for drumset that is based on the percussion instruments playing Afro-Cuban rhythms. The part instructs the bass to play a "tumbao". Tumbao is the bass part one would play in Afro-Cuban or Latin rhythm such as rumba, mambo, guaguanco or son. The basic part is this:

Example 28. Basic Tumbao

This would be a basic tumbao on the chord changes at letter **C**.

Example 29. Tumbao on Chords at Letter C

Now here is what the bass plays at letter C.

Example 30. Bass Part at Letter C

Notice how the bass part supports the piano. I spoke previously about deriving parts from different instruments. This is a great example. When playing Afro-Cuban grooves, you have many places to look for ideas, for example any of the percussion parts (conga, cowbell, cascara or clave), the vocal melodies, horns or piano parts. I heard Carlos Del Puerto, the great bassist for the Cuban super group Irakere speak to students at The Collective about getting many of his ideas from the piano parts. That opened up my mind because I had always listened more to the percussion instruments for ideas. Always keep your eyes and ears open because there are great rhythms you can use all around you.

After the form is played, the piano solos at letter **B** until cuing at letter **C**. From there we return to letter **A** for an open bass solo based on E minor. The term "open" solo means that it is not restricted to any amount of bars, and you are expected to give a cue to the band when you are finished and wish to move on. Open can also refer to the harmonic direction of your solo and how you define it. Here, although it's generally E with a minor sound, there are many options at your disposal, and Lincoln uses them. There is of course, E minor but you can also use pentatonic scales, the blues, altered scales, diminished patterns, Phrygian modes and chromatic notes. Basically, you can do whatever you want as long as it's musical, and sounds and feels good. That sounds like good criteria.

The bass solo uses the blues, pentatonic scales, diminished scales and dominant-altered scales expertly, and the solo has a real nice arc to it. In other words, it builds from being simple to busy, from lower register to upper register, and from simpler harmony to more complex harmony, coming to a nice climax before the cue for the riff at letter **A**. It takes experience and skill to be able to craft a solo as a complete statement instead of smaller groupings of ideas.

Well, you would think that after a great bass solo like that that we may as well just end the song and go home, right ? But no, there must be a drum solo, so we play letter **B** and take the coda, where we return to $\frac{6}{8}$ for the drum solo. Once again, we have a figure to play during the solo, so we must be on guard to keep our place and keep our rock-solid time. The figure is doubled up after a cue from the drummer and then, one last transition back to $\frac{4}{4}$ for the last two bars. The ritard at the end is, again, conducted by the drummer. Another important skill of a professional musician and something that I've always felt should be taught more in music schools is how to follow a conductor. Here, of course, the conductor is the drummer, but it's important to know how to follow a band leader's or conductor's direction and his motions while still playing and reading the music.

Monte Cristo
CD Track #5 Demo / Track #6 Play-along

Monte Cristo

LINCOLN GOINES and
BILL O'CONNELL

1st time D.S. to [B]
2nd time D.S.S. to [A]

Chart Roadmap
Intro, A (4x), B, C, D, B, C, D, A, B, Coda, E

CHAPTER 4:
[Ol' Factory]

Ol' Factory by Burr Johnson is a sixteenth-note Funk composition. It has a combination of groove sections along with some ensemble unison figures that highlight another important skill in the performance of this music. That is, the ability to go between playing time and playing figures smoothly and accurately. One of the really interesting things about this track is its ability to be funky without having a steady backbeat all the time. Kim Plainfield calls this kind of jam "sophistifunk," a more sophisticated and complex form, but still very funky. One of the classics of this style is Herbie Hancock's *Actual Proof* from the early 1970s. Here, your sense of time and pulse comes into play in a big way with the drums playing the snare on different beats and the band entering some sections in unison on beat 2. When the whole band plays an upbeat in unison or comes in strong on a beat other than 1, it can throw the listener's sense of pulse, not to mention the player's, so be careful to keep your groove sense together when making the accents and figures as well as the unison entrances.

This song is another good example of the variety of skills needed to perform at this level. It is a nice blend of reading and improvisation, where the bassist has written obligations that he must execute but also has some space to create and play on his own. I've chosen to include a transcription of what was played on the recording. This should be just a starting point for your creativity. Make sure your part is in perfect rhythmic alignment with the drums and guitar.

Let's start with the opening figure. It's common on lead sheets to have measures that have the chords within the bar lines with rhythmical accents written on top of the bars, showing you where to place the chords. It looks like this.

Example 31. Bars with Accented Chords

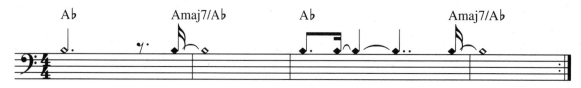

Now add to that a written figure every other bar and you have something similar to the opening of *Ol' Factory.*

Example 32. Accents with Figure

When playing accented chords in unison with the band, make sure not to rush the figures and pay attention to the rest of the band. Try this four-bar group of accents.

Example 33. A Four-Bar Pattern of Accents

After the two-bar guitar break, the opening groove is introduced, but with a figure every other bar played with the guitar, then a one-bar break before the melody begins. Al Payson plays a great variety of techniques in this song. The groove at letter **A** is a sixteenth-note funk groove. Playing this style requires good technique and coordination between your left and right hands, and good agility on your instrument. You're playing a lot of notes and if any of them are early or late, you'll stumble and disrupt the flow of the music. Notice how in the fifth bar of the melody, the whole band leaves beat 1 empty and comes in together on the "and" of beat 1. This creates the deception of a new downbeat momentarily and is a slick arranging technique.

Here are a couple of sixteenth-note exercises to get you going.

Example 34.

Example 35.

III Position

G7

III Position

G7 (alternative)

Now here's the bass part.

Example 36. Bass Part

In addition to playing the part on the CD, try to come up with your own groove with the rest of the rhythm section, maintaining the flavor of the song and the sixteenth-note feel.

Another great lesson in this performance is how to make transitions smoothly and accurately. With accents on different upbeats, some of the transactions between sections sound like there are extra beats or odd bars, but if you count, you will see that there is none. It's how the band is executing the accents that gives it that feel.

In bar 9, the groove and melody continue on the 4 chord, while the bass plays quarter notes in the last two bars before the transition. This smoothes things out before the next section, which is a brief restatement of the intro. This simple choice—to play two bars of quarter notes—is a great idea, reminiscent of one of my favorite bassists in the world, Anthony Jackson. If you pick the right spot, laying down some fat quarter notes in the middle of a syncopated funk groove can be a really great choice, but remember, only **if you pick the right spot.**

 The next section sounds like a bridge or interlude section; once again, there is a guitar melody pickup, and the band enters after beat 1, on the "and" of 1. Here, the bass part combines a quarter-note walking feel with some slaps and pops. When using the quarter-note feel, make sure you play long, fat notes with even attacks. Here is a combination quarter-note/slap exercise. Sometimes, I play parts that alternate between my fingers and slapping. Try that as well as all slap. It can be difficult to go back and forth between the two techniques.

Example 37. Quarter Notes with Slaps

Try your own part using the same technique on these changes.

Example 38. Chord Changes for Part Creation

The next melody starts with just the guitar for four bars. The band then enters and picks it up in bar 5, and we play out the section and proceed to the solos.

In the guitar solo section, once again the word "arc" or shape comes up. We have an even fuller sixteenth-note pattern with little rest, but great articulation. One of the great sixteenth-note funk players is Francis Rocco Prestia of Tower of Power, who sometimes would play straight sixteenth notes, with no rests. Here, the bass and drums are locked, and Al's steady sixteenth notes make a nice cushion for Kim's displaced snare hits. Also, the bass follows the arc of the solo really well, getting more active at the right times, listening to the guitar and supporting the music.

Here's one more sixteenth-note exercise, this time one with no rests and not much syncopation. What makes this funky and makes it work is the articulation, making the notes short and even. Try it.

Example 39. Sixteenth-Note Exercise with No Rests

This composition is very interesting because it has a lot of twists and turns. During the solo, there are accents and breaks, and even a drum solo between two guitar solo sections. Again, we're in a situation where we have to play a figure, a syncopated figure, to support the drum solo, so be diligent in your time, as always.

Example 40. Drum-Solo Figure

After another guitar solo, we return to the head but then play the second and final melody at a slower tempo to take the song out. *Ol' Factory* is a great example of the versatility of the musicians performing it and of the diverse skills that one needs to be a successful professional musician.

Class Notes: _____

_____

_____

Class Notes: _____

_____

_____

Class Notes: _____

_____

_____

Class Notes: _____

_____

_____

Class Notes: _____

_____

_____

These are the transcribed bass parts from the recording. Feel free to create your own lines; however, make sure you include the syncopated hits with the drums and guitar.

Ol' Factory
CD Track #7 Demo / Track #8 Play-along

Ol' Factory

BURR JOHNSON

Cool guitar scratch

Don't rit.!

rit.   *Fine*

Guitar solo first time; drum solo second time
(open solos cue D)

C   A♭

(Example line: start smooth and slick. Free free to improvise
your part or stick to an ostinato phrase.)

(Repeat to C)

D.S. to B al Fine

Chart Roadmap
Intro, A, B, C-D (2x), B

Discography

These recordings represent the various fusion styles. Not all album titles are named, only my favorites, but in most cases, any record made by these artists is not only representative, but also recommended.

Airto
Fingers
Free

Bill Bruford
Feels Good to Me
One of a Kind

Cannonball Adderly Quintet
Black Moses

Caribbean Jazz Project
Caribbean Jazz Project
Island Stories
New Horizons
Paraiso

Stanley Clark
Journey to Love
School Days
Stanley Clark

Billy Cobham
Crosswinds
Magic
Spectrum
Total Eclipse

Bill O'Connell
Black Sand
Lost Voices

Chick Corea
The Leprechaun
My Spanish Heart

Chick Corea and Return to Forever
Hymn of the Seventh Galaxy
Light as a Feather
Return to Forever
Where Have I Known You Before

Larry Coryell
Spaces

Miles Davis
Agartha
Bitch's Brew
In A Silent Way
Jack Johnson
Live Evil
On the Corner

George Duke
The Aura Will Prevail
Brazilian Love Affair
Feel

Herbie Hancock
Headhunters
Mr. Hands
Mwandishi
Thrust

The Mahavishnu Orchestra
Between Nothingness and Eternity
Birds of Fire
The Inner Mounting Flame
Visions of the Emerald Beyond

Tania Maria
Come with Me
Don't Go
Made in New York

Vince Mendoza
Epiphany
Sketches
Start Here

Pat Metheny
Bright Size Life
Pat Metheny Group
Still Life (Talking)

Marcus Miller
M
The Sun Don't Lie

Andy Narrell
Behind the Bridge
Live in South Africa
Passage

Hermeto Pascoal
Zabumbe-bum-a

Jaco Pastorius
Jaco Pastorius
Word of Mouth

John Pattitucci
Another World
Heart of the Bass
Mistura Fina
Sketch Book

Jean Luc Ponty
Enigmatic Ocean
Imaginary Voyage
Tchokola

Sakesho
Sakesho
We Want You to Say

Seis de Solar
Alternate Routes
Decision

Wayne Shorter
Atlantis
Native Dancer
Phantom Navigator

Samuel Torres
Skin Tones

The Yellow Jackets
Dreamland
Like a River
Politics

Ultramarine
e si mala

Dave Valentin
Kalahari
Live at the Blue Note

Weather Report
8:30
Black Market
Heavy Weather
Mysterious Traveler
Sweetnighter

Tony Williams Lifetime
Believe It
Emergency!

Joe Zawinul
Faces and Places
Zawinul

Some fusion style recordings that I've appeared on are:

Luis Bonilla
Escucha

Don Byron
You Are Number 6

The Collective
25th Anniversary DVD and concert CD

Joseph Diamond
Not Your Typical New Yorker
Island Garden

Peter Eldridge
Fool No More

Kenia
Project: Iven Lins

Machan
Machan

Mandara (Featuring Valarie Naranjo and Barry Olson)
Mandara

Tania Maria
The Lady from Brazil

Hendrik Meurkins
View from Manhattan

Gerry Mulligan with Jane Duboc
Paraiso

The New York Voices
The Music of Paul Simon
Skin
What's Inside

Mark Wagnon
Shadowlines

Chris Washburn and SYOTOS
The Land of Nod
Paradise in Trouble